Reflections

A Play in One Act

Colin and Mary Crowther

A Samuel French Acting Edition

FOUNDED 1830

SAMUELFRENCH.COM
SAMUELFRENCH-LONDON.CO.UK

Copyright © 2009 by Colin and Mary Crowther
All Rights Reserved

REFLECTIONS is fully protected under the copyright laws of the United States of America, the British Commonwealth, including Canada, and all other countries of the Copyright Union. All rights, including professional and amateur stage productions, recitation, lecturing, public reading, motion picture, radio broadcasting, television and the rights of translation into foreign languages are strictly reserved.

ISBN 978-0-573-12223-1

www.SamuelFrench.com
www.SamuelFrench-London.co.uk

For Production Enquiries

United States and Canada
Info@SamuelFrench.com
1-866-598-8449

United Kingdom and Europe
Theatre@SamuelFrench-London.co.uk
020-7255-4302

Each title is subject to availability from Samuel French, depending upon country of performance. Please be aware that *REFLECTIONS* may not be licensed by Samuel French in your territory. Professional and amateur producers should contact the nearest Samuel French office or licensing partner to verify availability.

CAUTION: Professional and amateur producers are hereby warned that *REFLECTIONS* is subject to a licensing fee. Publication of this play(s) does not imply availability for performance. Both amateurs and professionals considering a production are strongly advised to apply to Samuel French before starting rehearsals, advertising, or booking a theatre. A licensing fee must be paid whether the title(s) is presented for charity or gain and whether or not admission is charged. Professional/Stock licensing fees are quoted upon application to Samuel French.

No one shall make any changes in this title(s) for the purpose of production. No part of this book may be reproduced, stored in a retrieval system, or transmitted in any form, by any means, now known or yet to be invented, including mechanical, electronic, photocopying, recording, videotaping, or otherwise, without the prior written permission of the publisher. No one shall upload this title(s), or part of this title(s), to any social media websites.

For all enquiries regarding motion picture, television, and other media rights, please contact Samuel French.

MUSIC USE NOTE

Licensees are solely responsible for obtaining formal written permission from copyright owners to use copyrighted music in the performance of this play and are strongly cautioned to do so. If no such permission is obtained by the licensee, then the licensee must use only original music that the licensee owns and controls. Licensees are solely responsible and liable for all music clearances and shall indemnify the copyright owners of the play(s) and their licensing agent, Samuel French, against any costs, expenses, losses and liabilities arising from the use of music by licensees. Please contact the appropriate music licensing authority in your territory for the rights to any incidental music.

IMPORTANT BILLING AND CREDIT REQUIREMENTS

If you have obtained performance rights to this title, please refer to your licensing agreement for important billing and credit requirements.

PRODUCTION NOTES

The setting represents an hotel bedroom and adjoining bathroom, created simply and imaginatively, for example using different sized white cubes, seen against a dark curtained setting.

R is the bedroom. CR, angled outwards, there is a long white cube on legs with drawers painted onto it in shades of grey. This will serve as a dressing table. It has a white mirror frame above it. A small white cube is pulled up to it, painted to look padded. This will serve as a stool. DR –through the mirror as it were–is a black cube. C there is a long white cube painted in greys to look like an ottoman, standing at the foot of an unseen bed. (A luggage trestle in front of or behind the ottoman will be useful for the suitcase, and a 'headboard'' UC will help to give the effect of depth to the bed). Now imagine a line from UC to DC. This is the wall dividing bedroom from bathroom. On that wall, DC is the unseen door, above that a white, free-standing, full-length mirror frame, and above that a white coat stand.

L is the bathroom. ULC, two white cubes, one behind the other, are shaded in greys to look like a WC. LC, two more cubes, one on top of the other, angled outwards, look like a pedestal hand basin with a mirror frame above it. DSL–through the mirror as it were–is a tall black 'cube'. Between the loo and the hand basin stands a towel rail with a white towel on it. Together these items represent the bathroom.

There is a door to the bedroom CR, a door to the bathroom DC and a window to the bathroom UL above towel rail. These are all mimed. (Only where directed should any attempt be made for the reflections to mimic the movements of the people—we are dealing with alter egos—the mirrors show the main characters not so much what they are doing as what they are thinking and feeling).

The play is divided into scenes for use in rehearsal, each scene representing a new reflection and a chance to take stock and change gear and pace. But in performance, the scenes should flow together without a break. The play is followed by an optional Reprise. Even if you do not use it in performance, it could be useful to start rehearsals by reading it aloud as it gives the actors a quick overview of the emotional shape of the play.

Colin and Mary Crowther

O wad some Pow'r the giftie gie us
To see oursels as others see us!
                                    Robert Burns

Other plays by Colin and Mary Crowther, published by
                Samuel French Ltd:

Footprints in the Sand (Colin Crowther)
        The Lost Garden (full length)
        Noah's Ark (for children)
            Till We Meet Again
            Tryst (Colin Crowther)
                Just Passing

REFLECTIONS

Scene 1

She sits on the ottoman, dressed in a white towelling robe — clearly the property of the hotel — and white slippers with pink pom-poms, a ghastly gift from him, so she has to wear them. Her Reflection, looking frumpy in baggy greys, sits on the black cube DR *and watches her, adopting a very glum posture*

He sits on the loo, dressed in a white shirt and black socks, his white boxer shorts round his ankles. (For reasons which will soon become apparent, he may wish to wear black briefs and a shirt with long front and tail) His Reflection, looking smart and slim in greys, sits on the black cube DL *and watches him, but adopting a very jaunty posture*

She and He both stare glumly out front. Pause

Her Oh...flip!
Him Oh...heck!

Their Reflections spin to face out front

Her Reflection Mirror, mirror, on the wall...
His Reflection Who's the fairest of them all?
His Reflection }
Her Reflection } (*together*) Don't ask us or your face will fall!

They cackle like wicked old witches, then spin to face us *and remain very still, but in their original jaunty/gloomy postures. He and she start speaking, growing ever faster*

Him Oh heck.
Her Oh flip.
Him Oh heck.
Her Oh flip.
Him Oh heck.

Pause

Her What have I talked myself into?
Him What have I done?
Her I've always hated a fuss.
Him A dinner dance!
Her Perhaps I should have said.
Him She'll be expecting it. Slap-up do... dinner...dancing... speeches...
Her When he told me, I could have died!
Him But the look on her face!
Her I wanted the floor to open up and swallow me!
Him Made it all worthwhile!
Her I hate parties.
Him She's only ever been to three — in the whole of her life — I remember, she told me.
Her I walked out. Every time. I never planned to. I'd just be popping out for a breath of air, but somehow I'd keep going till I found myself back where I started—home.
Him She always had to leave early. So she missed out, poor thing.
Her Like the last one we went to.
Him My works Christmas do.
Her He got drunk.
Him Drop too much. Bit of a laugh, really.
Her I could have cried. Everyone looking. I swore to myself then...
Him Maybe I should have warned her.
Her You'd think he'd have realized.
Him Not sprung it on her like that. Surprise!
Her I nearly fainted.

Reflections 3

Him But tonight I'm determined. We're going to be the centre of attention.
Her I hate that!
Him I love that!
Her And they'll all be thinking, (*self-deprecatingly*) "How did he end up with her?"
Him (*proudly*) They'll think, "How did someone like him get someone like her?" (*Puzzled*) So why do I have this feeling that tonight ...
Her Tonight is going to be ...
Him ⎫
Her ⎭ (*together*) A disaster!

Pause

Him Oh heck!
Her Oh flip!

They both rise

Him Perhaps we can get away early.
Her We'll just have the meal.
Him And slip away during the dancing.
Her I hate dancing.
Him But I love dancing.

Simultaneously, she shuffles over to the long mirror C, her eyes glued on those stupid slippers that make walking so awkward and he shuffles over to the other side of the same mirror, shuffling because his shorts are still round his ankles. They look at their reflections in the mirror, and sigh

Her The thing about dancing...
Him The thing I really love...
Her Really hate...
Him Is that when I'm dancing, I feel like I'm walking on air. (*He twirls to demonstrate*)

Her Like an elephant on stilts. (*She twirls to demonstrate*)
Him I feel I can be anyone — the person I was always meant to be — Fred Astaire... John Travolta... (*He takes one foot out of his shorts and does a characteristic dance step in the style of one of his idols*)
Her But talking, just the two of us, lights down low — then I can sparkle, talk for hours, fly — I'm Audrey Hepburn... Julia Roberts...

He stops dancing

Him It's just making a speech I hate.
Her I hope he doesn't try to make a speech.
Him Only solution — get drunk first!
Her He'll get drunk, then nothing will stop him.
Him Like at the Christmas do. At work. Dead proud of that one.
Her His friends egg him on.
Him Great bunch of lads!
Her But he's the one who ends up looking a fool.
Him The look on the boss' face!
Her One more speech like that and he will lose his job.
Him He looked just like our old Headmaster!
Her Might be a good thing. It really doesn't suit him.
Him Funny, even then it was always them, egging me on. But always me getting caught.
Him
Her } (*together*) Maybe the time has come to move away.

Simultaneously, they move away from their mirrors, heading back for the ottoman or loo. He stops halfway, turns US, *lifts the front of his shirt and looks down*

Him Are you all right down there?

She stops halfway, turns DS, *and clutches her tummy*

Her Oh. I feel sick. Again.

Reflections

Him I'm sorry about last night. I should never have let the lads do that to you. I thought it would wash off by now.

She turns to look at the bathroom door

Her Do you think I should tell him?

He turns to look at the bathroom door

Him Do you think I should tell her?
Her No. Not now.
Him } (*together*) { I'll tell her tonight.
Her } { I'll tell him tonight.

She turns to cross to the dressing table. He pulls up his shorts

Her (*calling*) Are you all right in there?
Him (*calling*) I'll be out in a minute.

She sits at the dressing table. He crosses to the sink

Scene 2

Him }
Her } (*together*) It's too late to back out now.

Simultaneously, their Reflections start to move. Her Reflection swivels to face DR; *his to face* DL. *Once in position, Her Reflection mimes filing away at a broken finger nail, then giving up and biting it. His Reflection mimes patting aftershave onto his cheeks then smoothing it in. Meanwhile, the real "He" shaves with an electric razor. The real "She" paints her nails*

Her I wish Mum was here. Oh, it might not be too bad. Just another two, three hours... Aunty Jean's here... Friends from work... I'll be fine. Until the dancing. I can just about manage a waltz, if I count, out loud. More than that and I really come unstuck. Everyone watching... Oh, Lord, his boss!

Him At least Dad won't be there. Lads from work will! Hope they behave. Trouble is, when I'm with them, I feel I've got to play along — but it's always me ends up looking the fool. And I don't feel like Jack-the-Lad right now. Never did, to be honest. Oh, it'll be OK. I'll be fine. Until the speech. Everyone watching... Oh, Lord, I wish Mum was here!

Her (*calling*) Were you calling?

Him (*calling*) No. (*To himself*) We'll have to move away. But what would I do?

Her There's so much he could do.

Him I've always worked there — or somewhere like there.

Her He's wasted his life away in dead-end jobs.

Him Nothing else I'm fit for.

Her He could do anything he wanted, anything he set his mind to. He just needs someone to believe in him. It's all any of us wants, really.

Her Reflection Hark at her!

Him I'm nobody special.

His Reflection You don't want to be, mate.

Him I was special once. Till Mum died. Then I left school. Got in with the lads. Didn't seem to matter what I did after that. It was bound to go wrong, so why try?

Her I wish I could have met his mum.

Him I'll never be an auto mechanic now. Never own my own garage, like Uncle John... I'm just a salesman. Not a very good one. Selling second-hand cars... Not very good ones.

Her I wish I'd had the chance to tell her, "You don't need to worry about him now. I'll look after him. I've decided. It's all going to be fine..."

Him Can't go to college now.

His Reflection Who'd want to, anyway?

Him What would she think?

His Reflection You'll never know if you don't tell her.
Her Reflection Tell him.
Her What would he think?
Her Reflection You'll never know if you don't tell him.

Suddenly, he spins round to face the bathroom door. She rises and does the same. Then they lose courage

Her Maybe...
Him Later... If I can just get through the next few hours.
His Reflection Chicken.
Her (*calling*) Ready?
Him (*calling*) Chicken.
Her (*calling*) Pardon?
Him (*calling*) Not quite.
His Reflection }
Her Reflection } (*together*) Chicken!

Disappointed, Him and Her turn back to look into their mirrors

The Reflections swivel round to face DC. Pause

Scene 3

Him }
Her } (*together*) Will you just look at me!

She begins to touch up her make-up. He finishes shaving

Her Don't know why I'm bothering. Look at me. I'm a dowdy, boring frump.
Her Reflection True.
Her I look ten years older than him.
Her Reflection ... Also true.
Her They'll think I'm a cradle-snatcher.

Her Reflection With a zit.
Her Oh, no! It'll be like every party I've ever been to, all rolled into one. On my own. In the corridor. Tongue-tied, tripping over, trying not to look up, so I don't catch anyone's eye. Oh, what can I do?
Her Reflection Hara-kiri's popular.
Him Why do I always feel forty-two and look twenty-four?
His Reflection Because you listen to me.
Her Why do I always feel twenty-four and look forty-two?
Her Reflection Because you listen to me.

He pats on his aftershave

Him Tell me.
His Reflection She's a lucky girl.
Him More.
His Reflection You could have had anyone.
Him Still could.
His Reflection Life in the old dog yet.
Him Boom! Boom!
His Reflection Right.
Him Wrong. How long is it since I pulled? I mean actually pulled?
His Reflection (*pointing to Her*) You mean, before her?

He nods

What about Susan?
Him Susan, as I recall, said that if I were the last man in the entire solar system...
His Reflection Yes, well. She didn't know what she was missing.
Him But she did. I went out with Susan for six months.
His Reflection Remember that Christmas party?
Him Not really.
His Reflection Course you do! Sandra?
Him Was she the blonde with the tight top?

Reflections

His Reflection Brunette with baggy trousers.
Him Actually, I don't think...
His Reflection Well, let me colour in the bits that have gone blurry...
Him Must you?
His Reflection What I'm here for. Life and soul of the party you were. Out there, centre of the action...
Him You're making it up.
His Reflection What you pay me for.
Him Go on.
His Reflection Few drinks inside you, don't know what you can do.
Him That's the trouble. I was too drunk to remember.
His Reflection What it's all about.
Him Is it? I don't think I actually like beer. I don't think it agrees with me. And I hate whisky. It always makes me sick.
His Reflection You're not going soft on me, are you? Me old pal? Me old mate?
Him Buzz off.
His Reflection Right. Shan't tell you then.
Him Tell me what?
His Reflection You've got a zit.
Him Oh, no! (*He hurries to his side of the* C *mirror with his comb*)

She looks around at the dressing table area

Her It's very gloomy over here.
Her Reflection Charming!
Him I can't stand bright lights.

She takes her hairbrush to her side of the C *mirror*

His Reflection You'll miss me when I'm gone.
Her Surprised I didn't notice it before.
Her Reflection All the thanks I get.

They begin to do their hair, stopping every now and then to think and re-evaluate themselves in this, much clearer mirror

Her If Mum could see me now...

Him After Mum died, and Dad was back on the booze, the house felt very empty. There was always Uncle John. Nice bloke. Good of him to take an interest. Let me play around in his garage. Trouble is, he never shut up. Always full of advice, most of it rubbish. Still, he means well.

Her After Dad left and Mum married again, the place seemed very empty. Still, there was always Aunty Jean. Only really got her left now. And that's nice. Sometimes she'll talk — and she's got lots of advice, good advice — but mostly she just wants to listen. Nice, people like that.

Him I should have washed it.

Her Sprayed it. (*She tries to catch sight of her bottom and turns for a better view*) Oh, no! It's spreading. It's never been down there before. Another five years and I'll scrape the ground with it. I'll have to pull it along in a trolley. From Tesco's. What did I do to deserve it? Eat? Never enough. Drink? Hardly ever. Not like him. And look at him!

He catches sight of his bottom and turns to get a better view

Him Gorgeous.

His Reflection So why the glum face?

He gives up and walks to the centre of the bathroom

Him The thing I hate about selling used cars is the look they give you. It's either hard and "I wouldn't trust you if you told me the place was on fire" — I can outstare them any day — or appealing and "I don't know about cars. I have to hope you're telling me the truth. Can I trust you?" But what I really hate about selling cars is I can't look them in the eye when I have to say, "Oh, this is a great car. Trust me."

She turns and walks to the centre of the bedroom then turns back

Reflections

Her I remember telling Aunty Jean about this place where I work. Beautiful Victorian house it is. Offices now. But as you walk down the panelled hall and watch the light from the stained glass window playing on the walls like a giant kaleidoscope, you can still get a feel of what it must have been like to live there and rustle down the staircase in your crinoline. In the end, it's not about totting up the figures, building up the expenses, cutting down the taxes. It's about painting a dream. 'Cause that's what they want, our clients. We panel the walls with tax relief and stain the windows with stocks and shares, all so our clients can float down the staircase of a dream they can trust.

Him Cars are still a dream for people. Power. Strength. "Look what I've got—and such a shiny colour!" Big sports jobs. Little runabouts. "As long as I've got a car, I've got my independence." Family cars. "Look what a great dad I am — the sacrifice I made —I could have had as sports car, girl on each arm . No. I'm playing safe, and all for the wife and kids." Comes down to the same thing. They don't want a car. They want a dream. A dream they can trust.

She walks back to the mirror C

Her Sometimes I get to take the figures through to the Conference Room, and there they sit, a man and his wife, an ordinary couple who run their own little shop, their own little show, and I think, "How lovely... how perfect to have a dream you can share!"

He walks back to the mirror C

Him And they bring their partner, and she looks and he looks, then they look at each other and... there's so much hope in their eyes, hope that this time the dream will come true, this dream they share.

Him
Her } (*together*) I wish we could share a dream like that.

Him That's why I want to mend things. Things that are broken. Put them right. So I can say, "Look, it works now. You CAN trust me!" And really look them in the eye. And smile.

Her He's got such a lovely smile. And he knows so much about cars. Sometimes, I think he's trying to sell me one. But the only time I said to him, "I do need a car", he said, "Well, don't look at me!"

Scene 4

He steps close to the mirror

Him Whatever does she see in me?

His Reflection Don't ask me. You're heading for forty, you've got a zit— and you're going bald!

Him Oh, no!

She steps up close to the mirror. They resume work on their hair

Her I'm not his type at all. I'm not anyone's. Mum was right.

Her Reflection (*quoting Mum*) " You'll end up round-shouldered and fat —just like your Aunty Jean."

Her But I like Aunty Jean. Only woman I know who looks happy being her — and let the world go hang. Funny, I was thinking of her when I first met him. (*She turns* DS *and smiles, contentedly*)

Him I remember the first time I saw her — sitting there, smiling, a sort of secret smile, like she could see through the whole world and still find something to smile about. I asked her to dance.

Her He said, "Dance?" I said, "No. There are far better things to do than dancing."

Him I thought, oh yeah? Scored here, me old mate. In for a night of...

Her Talking.

Him So we talked. All night.

Her I like talking. What I don't like is what hairdressers do to your hair! (*She flings her brush at the dressing table*)

He looks at his comb

Him Oh, heck! It's true! I am going bald! (*He crosses to the loo, presses the flush button*)

The lavatory flushes

He sits

She becomes aware of how long he has been in there

Her Haven't you finished yet?
Him I've only just started!
Her We're going to be late.
Him We'll be very much later if I keep stopping to tell you I've only just started! Honestly.
Her Men!
Him Women!

Very puzzled, and slightly worried now, she goes to sit on the ottoman. She crosses her legs one way, then the other way

Scene 5

Her I'll just have to make the best of it.
Him How did we get from that to this?
Her It just snowballed.
Him From one night of talking to a lifetime of ...What?
Her Whatever will we talk about?
Him No good. I'll just have to make the best of it.
Her Or make a run for it.

Simultaneously, they both double take. He climbs on the loo and tries the window, high in the wall beside it, out of our sight. She runs for the bedroom door. Then they both turn and look at the bathroom door and think of their partner. He comes to the bathroom door, then notices the clothes hanging from the coat stand

Him Oh, heck. (*Calling*) Er, excuse me...
Her Oh, flip. (*Calling*) Yes?
Him Excuse me, can I come out yet?
Her (*panicking*) Why?
Him Only, you've got my clothes out there, and I've got yours in here.
Her Let me think about it. (*She comes to the centre of her room and realizes he is right*)

Her Reflection moves to face her direction

Her Reflection Remember Aunty Jean?
Her What was it she said? About marriage? Going wrong? "The worst quality to have in a husband is imagination."
Her Reflection She was right.
Her She said they're always wondering "What if..." and it's only two steps from that to wondering when the next bus goes there. I don't understand that.
Her Reflection You will.
Her I'd have thought imagination was quite... Oh, I see... Well, good job he hasn't got any, then.

His Reflection moves to face his direction

His Reflection Remember Uncle John?
Him He was funny. He said the worst quality to have in a wife was an unforgiving nature.
His Reflection He was right.
Him He said, "There'll come a time when what you'll need is a little understanding and a lot of forgiving. And a man needs to know, when he comes clean, when he lays his eggs on the table, that the judge will be merciful and not scramble them..."
His Reflection And?
Him And "never do anything you don't want her to find out — because she will."
His Reflection Makes you think.

Her Reflection And?
Her Oh, and if you make like you know what he's been up to, it works. You will. It doesn't take a lot of work, because without imagination, it's only, betting, booze and birds. She taught me a sentence. How did it go?

Her Reflection rises, arms akimbo, a wronged wife on the warpath

Her Reflection "Where do you think you've been? As if I don't know. You needn't think you're sharing my bed after what you've been up to. And what do you think we'll do for money now?" (*Proudly, she sits*) Covers it all, one way or the other.
His Reflection Think. What else did he say?
Him That was about it, really. Oh, yes.

His Reflection rises and lectures him, resting one foot on his stool

His Reflection "When you think she's found out, stop lying, start praying."
Him (*remembering*) "Tell the truth."
His Reflection "Even if you don't tell all of it, tell enough so you can remember your story the day after. 'Cause sure as eggs is eggs, she will."
Him He's got a thing about eggs, has Uncle John.
Her In a way I don't mind what he does so long as he doesn't lie about it.
Him Daft, really. I can lie my way out of a paper bag.

His Reflection shakes his head

   She's never caught me yet.
His Reflection You've never lied to her. Yet.
Him Oh, what have I been doing then?
His Reflection Boasting. And no woman takes that seriously.
Her When you come down to it, the only ring that binds us — all we really have — is trust, and if I can't trust him over a little thing, how will I ever know I can trust him over a big thing?

Him Thing is...
Her Never lie.
Him Why should I want to?

Simultaneously, they turn and make for the bathroom door. They try the handle, in mime, but because they are both holding it, it won't budge

   Are you still there?
Her Oh. Right. Swap.

She adopts an alluring posture. He enters the bedroom and walks straight past her

Him Aren't you ready yet?

Furious, she goes into the bathroom and slams the door. She turns back to glare at the door. Too late, he realises he has missed his chance. He comes back to the door

Him Er...
Her Too late. You'll have to wait... You will wait?
Him Not half! (*He crosses and sits on the ottoman, rummaging through the suitcase and pulling out his ties*) She's got lovely eyes. Sometimes she looks at me, looks right deep inside me, and her eyes say...
Her Reflection "I'm going to trust you. I'm going to give you all my trust. You'd better not let me down."
Him No, that's not it. "And I know you won't let me down." That's it. One look from her can blow me clean away.
Her Reflection Look at me.

He tries, but turns away at the last minute

Him I'm no good with eyes. I can't say things with my eyes. It's that damn job, having to lie all day. Instead, I smile. (*He rises*)
Her Reflection Lovely smile.
Him I let my smile say, "I'll try. I really will try. With heart and soul I'll try." (*He crosses to the dressing table with his ties*)
Her Reflection You going to wear all of those?

Scene 6

He lays out his ties on the dressing table

Him I'll just have to make the best of it.
Her It's not as though I don't want to.
Him I do.

She comes to the centre of the bathroom

Her I will.
Him And we did.

They hold themselves in an imaginary embrace. The trouble is, he adds kissing sounds — loud kissing sounds. She looks up

Her What was that?
Him Nothing.
Her Who are you talking to?
Him No one... Myself!
Her I really worry about him sometimes.

He comes to the dressing table and admires himself. The mirrors swivel round to face DL/DR. *She busies herself at the sink*

Him She is such a lucky girl.
Her Reflection My heavens, will you look at yourself! How old are you? Really?

Him Twenty, in the shade.
Her Reflection More like forty.
Him Anyway, I can still pull. This afternoon. Tandy. Gave me the glad eye.
Her Reflection Hadn't got her glasses on. Thought you were your mate, Dave.
Him I don't look a bit like Dave!
Her Reflection Yes, you do. You're both going thin on top.
Him No, I'm not!
Her Reflection Turn round. Yup. Practically bald.
Him Oh, heck!
Her Reflection Truth is, you were lucky to get her — and you know it!
Him I do, I do! (*He sits, deflated, at the dressing table*)
Her Trouble is, I'm just not good enough for him!
His Reflection Hiya, sexy. Give me a twirl. Grrrr! Come with your older sister, did you? Thought so. You're too young to be out on your own.

She laughs aloud. He reacts

Her As if. I'm nearly thirty.
His Reflection He's nearly forty.
Her He never!
His Reflection Well, thirty-four.
Her He told me——
His Reflection Men for you.
Her But I *feel* so old! Look at these lines!
His Reflection Character.
Her And these.
His Reflection Yow!
Her And this.
His Reflection Boom-di-di-boom!
Her I'm spreading — all over the place.
His Reflection I know three lads downstairs who'd say, "You can spread in my direction, any day!"
Her Silly...Who?
His Reflection His pals from work.

Her Daft... Dave's nice.
His Reflection Going bald.
Her I like that in a man. Shows maturity. Virility.
His Reflection With a figure like yours, you won't have any trouble on that score.

She twirls again

Her I'm still not sure.
His Reflection Trust me.
Her Still, I must admit.
His Reflection Boom-di-di-boom!
Her The light *is* better over here.
His Reflection Truth is, he was lucky to get you — and he knows it.

She applies lipstick and blows a kiss at the mirror

Him Trouble is, I'm just not good enough for her!
Her Reflection True.
Him She could have had anyone!
Her Reflection Also true.

He sags, despondently

But she chose you.

He looks up

Him Hey! That makes me special, yeah?
Her Reflection That makes you lucky.

But he refuses to be deflated

Him (*to her mirror*) Who loves ya, sexy?
Her Reflection (*to Him*) You do.
Her I'd better get dressed.
His Reflection Don't want to keep him waiting.
Him I'd better get dressed.

Her Reflection Or she might not wait.

He takes his suit from the coat stand and takes it to the ottoman where he gets into it, facing upstage, so as not to distract attention from her. She takes a step back to check her make-up in the mirror

His Reflection What do you see in him? I mean, you could have had anyone.
Her He's shy. Underneath. He's like a mint with a soft, gooey centre.
His Reflection And women like that in a man?
Her I do.
His Reflection I still don't see it.
Her Ah well, that's love; what love is: seeing what no one else can see and knowing that's the real him.
His Reflection (*shaking his head*) He's a very lucky man.
Her Yes, he is. (*Suddenly, she is smiling, relaxed and confident for the first time since we have met her and suddenly we see what he sees in her*)

Over in the bedroom, he is struggling into his trousers

Her Reflection Nice bum.
Him It was. Now, suddenly, there's too much of it and it won't all fit. Like my waist. Do you think they shrink things — at the dry cleaners?
Her Reflection (*shaking her head*) It's what they call age, creeping up on you, from behind.
Him That's a sobering thought.
Her Reflection Good. 'Cause I've a question for you.
Him Sounds ominous. (*He goes over to the dressing table mirror and does a twirl*)

She goes to the coat stand and looks through the dresses hanging there

Her Reflection Let's pretend. You could have any woman in the world.
Him Wow!
Her Reflection I said "pretend"!

He fastens the top button of his shirt and raises his collar

Him If I could have any woman in the world...
Her Reflection Who would you choose?
Him Her.
Her Reflection Sure?
Him Every time.
Her Reflection Why? What's so special about her?
Him She's kind — and sexy — and cuddly. Bewitching, that's the word.
Her Reflection Nice word.
Him I feel I could love her all my life and never get bored. She's everything I could ever want — friend, lover, confidante — my better half.
Her Reflection I've news for you.
Him Oh, yes?
Her Reflection You're the only one.
Him Good. 'Cause d'you really think — if she knew she had a choice — of anyone else at all — she'd still have chosen me?
Her Reflection Try telling her that.
Him Oh, I couldn't.
Her Reflection Try.
Him She'd laugh at me.
Her Reflection You don't know her very well, do you?
Him To be honest, I don't really know women very well. I know the outside, not what goes on inside.
Her Reflection Lesson One. No woman laughs at being called bewitching.
Him I'll remember that.
Her Reflection No, you won't. The trouble with men is things sink in very slowly. Then keep on sinking.

Him Sorry—what did you say?
Her Reflection Glug, glug, glug.

He begins to choose a tie by holding them up in turn in front of the mirror. In the bathroom, she is working through the dresses in front of the c mirror with increasing anxiety and despair

Her Wonder if there's time to pop out to the hairdresser? No time. Never enough time. Why is it, the older you get the less time you have?
His Reflection Because the older you get the less time there is.

She shivers

Her Dress.
Him I was thinking. About that dress.
Her I was looking for weeks.
Him Getting more and more worked up. More and more depressed.
Her In the end, he said...
Him ...I'll go with you.
His Reflection Mistake.
Her I tried three on.
Him I said, "Great".
Her I said, "Which?"
Him I said, "Any".
Her Reflection Big mistake.
Him What was I supposed to say?
Her Reflection Which one you liked her in best.
Him Well, none of them, really. All a bit dull, a bit ordinary.
Her One was quiet, modest, subdued.
Him More like wallpaper.
Her One was calm, smart and sensible.
Him Like a schoolteacher.
Her And one...
Him ...I liked that one!

Her I looked like a whore's day out to Blackpool!
Her
Her Reflection } (*together*) Men!
Her In the end, I bought all three.
Him
His Reflection } (*together*) Women!
Him There was one there — on a dummy — I don't think she even saw it — really sophisticated — like she is, inside.
Her I'm more a paper bag and bin liner sort of person, really.
Her Reflection Did you tell her?
Him We weren't speaking by then.
Her Next day, I took the tart's dress back. And found another one. Really sophisticated, like I'd always wished I could be.
His Reflection Where is it?
Her Oh, I couldn't wear that.

He holds up three ties. She looks at her dresses

Him I can't decide.
Him
Her } (*together*) Which one to wear.
Him I've got this one with the pattern.
Her Reflection And the gravy stain.
Her This?
His Reflection Wallpaper.
Him Damn. Or this — you know — like a joke?
Her Reflection Bad joke.
Her Or this?
His Reflection School wallpaper.
Her Reflection Is that it?
His Reflection Where's number three?
Him Well, there is the one she bought me.
Her Reflection Where is it?
Her In the case.
His Reflection Fetch it.
Her But—

Her Reflection Now.

The couple converge on the suitcase. He takes out his tie, she a bundle of tissue paper

Him Hi.
Her Hello.
Him What's that for?
Her In case I want to blow my nose.
Him Oh.

By the time he double takes she has gone

Her Reflection Nice.
Him Oh, yes. (*Calling*) Are you going to be much longer? Only we don't want to be ──

She slams the door

Her Me? Late!
His Reflection Ignore him, show me.

She takes a dress out of the tissue paper

Her There!
His Reflection Yes!
Her I couldn't.
His Reflection You could.
Her I could.
His Reflection You show him.
Her I'll show him. (*She starts to put on the dress*)

He puts on the tie

Him Well?
Her Reflection Hang on. (*She reaches through the mirror frame and adjusts the knot on his tie*)

Her Do me up.

His Reflection rises, reaches through the mirror and helps her finish getting into the dress

His Reflection
Her Reflection } (*together*) There!

Scene 8

They stand and face each other through the C mirror. She is still clutching the tissue paper

Her I still don't feel good enough.
Him I suppose if *she* thinks I'm good enough.
Her So long as *he* thinks I am.
Her Reflection Shoes. Cufflinks.
His Reflection Shoes. Necklace.

This necessitates them changing rooms again. She opens the bathroom door and poses alluringly there. But there are problems. One, she has a huge bundle of tissue paper blocking his view of the dress in all its glory. Two, he is missing one shoe which he can't find because it is still in the case and one cufflink which is nowhere to be seen

Her Well?
Him Are you sure — I mean really sure — you need all those tissues? (*He passes her and limps, wearing one shoe, into the bathroom to search for the cufflink at the sink*)

She remains in the doorway, temporarily speechless

Her I have often wondered, when you read about it in the papers, what it was those husbands must have said to make their wives take a hatchet to them.

He is too busy searching to really be listening

Him Oh? What was that then?
Her What do I look like in this dress?

He turns, his face aglow

Think carefully before you speak.
Him Found it! Sorry, were you saying something?
Her Yes, that was probably it. (*She throws the tissue paper aside and storms over to the ottoman*)
Him Can you do my cufflinks? (*He picks up the paper and follows her*)
Her What do you think?
Him I don't know, that's why I'm asking. Oh! Wow! The dress. It's the same dress!
Her What do you mean? What's wrong with it?
Him The one the dummy was wearing. It looked great on the dummy.

The man is clearly a congenital idiot and she treats him as such

Her But how does it look on me?
Him Nice.
Her Nice? Nice!
Him Really nice. How about me?
Her Nice!
Him Oh. (*He puts the paper in the case and finds his missing shoe in there*)

She puts on her shoes, then decides they are the wrong ones. She searches for more in the case. He sits beside her, the case between them, and they put on their shoes in complete silence

Have I done something wrong?
Her I don't know. Have you?

Him Sorry. (*He holds out his hand for her to do the cufflink*)

She looks at him, thinking this is a sign of repentance, then slaps his hand, deciding it is not

Him Now will you do my cufflink?
Her Idiot.

She does the cufflink. He holds onto her hand

Him Only to be expected.
Her Why's that?
Him I'm in love.
Her Good. So am I. (*Fastening the other cufflink*)
Him Ready?
Her Almost.

SCENE 9

Their Reflections swivel back to face DC. *He takes his jacket, goes back into the bathroom and puts it on. She breaks to the dressing table, sits and puts on her necklace, then looks into the mirror*

His Reflection Here's looking at you, kid.
Him Will I do?
His Reflection The lady seems to think so.
Him That's all that matters, then.
His Reflection For once, we agree!
Her What do you think?
Her Reflection You scrubbed up well.
Her Cheeky! And him? I wonder what he really thinks.
Her Reflection "Who's a lucky boy, then!"
Her For once, we agree! (*She starts packing the case, then suddenly stops*) Do you realise, that's the first time we've agreed on anything?

He reaches the bathroom doorway and suddenly stops, turns back and looks at the bathroom mirror

Him Funny, we're normally on opposite sides.
Her Opposites...

Their Reflections swivel round till they are facing DR/DL. He positions himself between both bathroom mirrors, but facing the C mirror. She stands and crosses to C mirror. He holds up his left hand, she holds up her right

Him　⎫
Her　⎭ (*together*) What hand am I holding up?
His Reflection　⎫
Her Reflection　⎭ (*together*) Can't see.
Him　⎫
Her　⎭ (*together*) Try.

Their Reflections swivel back to face C, peering myopically through their mirrors

His Reflection Left.
Her Reflection Right.
Him　⎫
Her　⎭ (*together*) Wrong.

Triumphantly, they move closer to C mirror then turn and face their enemies

Her All this time you've told me the opposite–
Him What I wanted to hear, not what was really true.
Her Reflection I'm a reflection. What else could I do?
His Reflection If you prick us, do we not bleed?
Her No.
Her Reflection If you tickle us, do we not laugh?
Him No.
Her Why do you always look on the dark side?
Him The bright side?

Her Reflection What I'm here for.
Him Hang on. You're like a mirror, aren't you?
His Reflection Oh, give the lad a medal!
Her So you show me——
Her Reflection A true reflection.
Him What hand am I holding up?

They raise their right hands

His Reflection ⎫
Her Reflection ⎭ *(together)* Left.

Him ⎫
Her ⎭ *(together)* Right.

Her That's not the truth. That's the opposite!
Her Reflection Well, I'll go to the end of our lane!
Her And don't come back!
Him Ever! From now on, when I want an opinion, I'll ask——
Her Him...
Him —Her.
Him After all, that's what togetherness is about.
His Reflection *(rising)* If you shatter us, do we not break?
Her Reflection *(rising)* No! A thousand years' bad luck!
His Reflection Oh yes. Forgot that. OK. If you ——

Him ⎫
Her ⎭ *(together)* Oh, shut up!

Their Reflections sit, defeated. But he turns to face through the c *mirror, and so does she. They look into each others' eyes*

Now I have one mirror I know I can trust.

She raises her right hand. He mirrors her action with his left hand. Then they spread their fingers and hold them only a fraction apart, as if on either side of the thinnest pane of glass. Then they close their eyes and kiss, their faces just a fraction apart. Then they smile, turn to face out, and open their eyes

Her I look a million dollars!
Him I am so sexy!

He takes the toiletries bag to the suitcase. She takes her cosmetic and jewellery bags to the suitcase, where they meet and briefly kiss

Him
Her } (*together*) Wow!
Him I've got news for you.
Her Oh?
Him You look wonderful.
Her You look gorgeous.
Him I want to go to college and train to be an auto mechanic.
Her I'm so glad.
Him You don't mind?
Her We'll manage.
Him I'll need to get apprenticed.
Her Ask your Uncle John.
Him Oh, I'm not sure if——
Her Tell him, I'll do his books, for free. Who knows, one day——
Him Frobisher and Frobisher.
Her I was thinking more... Frobisher and Son...
Him Oh, no! (*He rises*)

She is dismayed. She rises

Her I thought you wanted a child?
Him Not one. I want girl-boy-girl, boy-boy-girl, two dogs and a hamster.

She sits, exhausted, counting them off on her fingers

Her I'll see what I can do.
Him Frobisher and Frobisher, a Family Company!

They sigh

His Reflection ⎫
Her Reflection ⎬ (*together*) Ah!
Him Ready?
Her As I ever will be.
Him Come on. We'd better put them out of their misery down there.
Her We said we'd only be quarter of an hour. They'll think...

They rise

Him Let's go and cut the cake.
Her Then we'd better get started on that list of yours.
Him We'll slip out when they start dancing.
Her We'll have to stay for one dance.
Him Let's make it a waltz.
Her Oh, yes. Are you all right about your speech?
Him I'll keep it short.
Her No jokes?
Him I don't want to make a complete fool of myself.
Her You could never do that.
Him Really? Oh, well, maybe just one.
Her Ready, Mr Frobisher?
Him Steady, Mrs Frobisher.

They link arms and go to the bedroom door, CR

Her It was a perfect wedding. Now let's make it a perfect marriage.

They kiss briefly and go out to face the world

Their Reflections swivel round to face each other, rise, lean through the mirror frames, and blow each other a kiss

Quick fade to Black-out

The End?

So that's what happened in front of their mirrors, but as we know, mirrors get things back to front. If you want to show how it probably really happened, you could try this...

REPRISE

You could start in the darkness with the pre-recorded voice of His Reflection making this announcement

His Reflection So that's what happened, or is it? We all know that mirrors can distort what we see, so what really happened in that hotel room just last Saturday? Perhaps it went like this...

Lights come up on Him sitting on the loo, Her sitting on the ottoman, the suitcase open beside her. Both of them are fully dressed. Their Reflections face upstage

Her Oh...flip!
Him Oh, heck!

Their Reflections turn to face UR/UL

Her Reflection What have I talked myself into?
His Reflection A dinner dance? It'll be a disaster.
Him Oh, heck!
Her Oh, flip!

He rises. She rises

Her Reflection I hate dancing!
His Reflection But I love dancing!

He comes to C *of the bathroom, she to* C *of the bedroom. They demonstrate their famous John Travolta/elephant on stilts dance steps*

His Reflection ⎫
Her Reflection ⎬ (*together*) Maybe the time has come to move away?

She clutches her tummy, he his crotch

Her I feel sick.
Him I'm so, so sorry.
His Reflection ⎫
Her Reflection ⎬ (*together*) It's too late to back out now.

He crosses to the sink to check his shaving has left a smooth chin. She crosses to the dressing table and checks her make-up is perfect. Their Reflections turn to face DC. *He makes kissing sounds*

His Reflection Anyway, what would you do?
Her There's so much he could do. He just needs someone to believe in him. It's all any of us wants really.
His Reflection Too late to go to college now. Never have your own garage now.
Her Reflection Whereas you are a dowdy, boring frump.
Her With a zit!
Him And going bald!

They break to C *mirror and as they look in it, their moods change. They begin to dream*

Him Frobisher...
Her And Frobisher.
Him I fix the cars...
Her I fix the books.

Their Reflections turn to face DR/DL

Him \
Her / (*together*) I wish we could share a dream like that!
His Reflection \
Her Reflection / (*together*) You'll just have to make the best of it.
Her Reflection Or make a run for it.

He dashes to bathroom window UL, *she to bedroom door,* CR. *They turn back*

Him Oh, heck.
Her Oh, flip.

Slowly, they walk towards the bathroom door

His Reflection What are you talking about?
Her Reflection It's not as though you don't want to.
Him \
Her / (*together*) I do.

They swap rooms, smiling shyly. When the bathroom door is closed, they lean against it, then come to C *of their new room and hug themselves romantically. He makes occasional kissing sounds. Their Reflections turn to face out through their mirror frames*

His Reflection Are you sure you're good enough for him?
Her Boom-di-di-boom!
Her Reflection You're just not good enough for her.

He pauses in the midst of a kiss

Him True. But she chose me. That makes me special.

They all turn to face him

His Reflection
Her Reflection } (*together; with great emphasis*) That makes you lucky!

Offended, he completes the kiss, realizes his cufflink is missing and heads for the suitcase. She realizes her scarf is missing and heads for the suitcase. They converge on the ottoman. She takes out a chiffon scarf

Him You scrubbed up well. (*Dashing off to the bathroom for one last check*)

She is crossing back to the dressing table when she double-takes at what he has said

Their Reflections slap their foreheads in horror at his gaffe and, still sitting, spin on their stools, ending up facing UL/UR

In the bathroom mirror he checks his tie is properly knotted

Her John Frobisher, get out here, now!
Him Let's go cut the cake.
Her The cake... can wait!

They fall into each other's arms. Their Reflections dance for joy around their stools

Black-out

CURTAIN

FURNITURE AND PROPERTY LIST

On stage: In bedroom
Dressing table. *On it*: nail polish, hair brush, cosmetics bag containing make-up, lipstick, jewellery bag containing necklace. *Above it*: white mirror frame
Stool (white)
Stool (black)
Ottoman. *In front of it*: man's shoe, pair of ladies shoes
Luggage trestle. *On it*: suitcase containing two dresses generously wrapped in tissue paper, three ties, recently removed man's suit, a male shoe
Bedhead
Coat stand. *On it*: man's suit on bedroom side, several dresses and ladies shoes on bathroom side

In bathroom
Cubes to form WC
Cubes to form hand basin. *On it*: toothbrush, electric shaver (nonprac.), toiletries bag containing aftershave, one cufflink. *Above it*: mirror frame
Tall black cube
Towel rail. *On it:* white towel

NOTE: There should be no wedding giveaways, like a bride's dress or confetti, anywhere in sight.

LIGHTING PLOT

To open: Cover spots DL and DR. Bright general interior lighting

Cue 1   Their Reflections blow each other a kiss   (Page 32)
              Quick fade to Black-out

REPRISE

To open: Darkness

Cue 2   **His Reflection**: "Perhaps it went like this..." (Page 32)
              Lights came up

Cue 3   Their Reflections dance for joy around their   (Page 35)
              stools
              Black-out

EFFECTS PLOT

Cue 1	He crosses to the loo and presses the flush button *Toilet flushing, quietly*	(Page 13)
Cue 2	She goes into the bathroom and slams the door *Door slam*	(Page 16)
Cue 3	She slams the door *Door slam*	(Page 24)

www.ingramcontent.com/pod-product-compliance
Lightning Source LLC
Chambersburg PA
CBHW070453050426
42450CB00012B/3250